The Power of Choice: Empowering Everyone's Decision-Making

Jack Roy

Title: The Power of Choice: Empowering Everyone's Decision-Making
Making
Author's: Jack Roy

This book was printed and published by [Publisher's: **Jack Roy**] in [2023]

ISBN:

TABLE OF CONTENT

Chapter 10: Conclusion 63

Chapter 1: Introduction to Decision-Making

The Importance of Decision-Making

In our day-to-day lives, we are faced with countless decisions, both big and small. From choosing what to wear in the morning to deciding on a career path, our lives are shaped by the choices we make. This subchapter delves into the significance of decision-making and how it can empower everyone to lead fulfilling lives.

Decision-making is an essential aspect of our existence. It allows us to assert control over our lives and shape our own destinies. By making thoughtful and informed choices, we can align our actions with our values and aspirations. Whether it's choosing a college major or deciding on a business strategy, decision-making enables us to pursue paths that resonate with our true selves.

Moreover, decision-making is a skill that can be honed and developed. By becoming adept at making decisions, we can navigate through life's challenges more effectively. Decision-making involves analyzing options, considering consequences, and weighing different possibilities. It helps us evaluate risks and rewards, ensuring that we make choices that lead to positive outcomes.

Making decisions is not always easy, as it often involves uncertainty and potential risks. However, avoiding decisions can be even more detrimental. Indecision can lead to missed opportunities, stagnation, and a sense of powerlessness. By embracing decision-making, we take control of our lives and open ourselves up to new possibilities.

Furthermore, decision-making is not just an individual endeavor; it affects those around us as well. Our choices impact our families, friends, colleagues, and communities. By making thoughtful decisions, we can positively influence and inspire others. We become role models for those in our spheres of influence, encouraging them to make choices that align with their values and aspirations.

In conclusion, decision-making is of utmost importance in our lives. It empowers us to take charge, pursue our dreams, and shape our futures. By developing our decision-making skills, we can navigate through life's challenges with confidence and clarity. Moreover, our choices have a ripple effect, influencing those around us in significant ways. So, let us embrace the power of decision-making and make choices that align with our true selves, ultimately leading us to a life of fulfillment and purpose.

Understanding the Power of Choice

In our journey through life, we are constantly faced with decisions to make. Some decisions may seem trivial, such as what to have for breakfast or which movie to watch, while others may be life-altering, like choosing a career path or deciding to start a family. Regardless of their magnitude, every decision we make has the power to shape our future.

Understanding the power of choice is essential in navigating through life's uncertainties and challenges. It empowers us to take control of our own destiny and create the life we desire. Each decision we make is an opportunity for growth and self-discovery, allowing us to learn from our mistakes, explore new possibilities, and shape our personal and professional paths.

Making decisions is not always easy. We often find ourselves at crossroads, torn between different options, or paralyzed by fear of making the wrong choice. However, the key to effective decision-making lies in understanding that choices are not simply a matter of right or wrong. Each decision we make carries with it potential opportunities and outcomes, and it is up to us to weigh the pros and cons, consider our values and priorities, and listen to our intuition.

The power of choice extends beyond our individual lives; it also has a ripple effect on those around us. Our decisions can inspire and motivate others, or they can negatively impact those we care about. Recognizing the influence our choices have on others encourages us to make decisions that align with our values and have a positive impact on our communities.

In this chapter, we will explore the various aspects of decision-making and delve into strategies for making informed and empowered choices. We will examine the role of intuition, the importance of considering long-term consequences, and the art of decision-making in complex situations. Additionally, we will discuss the power of reflection and learning from our decisions to continuously refine our decision-making skills.

No matter where you are in life or what your goals may be, understanding the power of choice is crucial. By embracing the responsibility and opportunity that comes with decision-making, you can unlock your full potential, create a life of purpose and fulfillment, and inspire others to do the same.

Join us on this transformative journey as we explore the intricacies of decision-making and discover the power that lies within each and every one of us. Together, let's embrace the power of choice and empower ourselves and those around us to make decisions that shape a brighter future.

Chapter 2: The Psychology of Decision-Making

Cognitive Biases and Decision-Making

In the realm of decision-making, our minds are not as rational as we may believe them to be. We are all prone to cognitive biases, which are inherent flaws in our thinking processes that can skew the way we perceive and evaluate information. These biases can greatly impact our decision-making abilities, leading us astray from making optimal choices. Understanding and recognizing these biases is crucial in empowering everyone's decision-making process.

One of the most common cognitive biases is the confirmation bias. This bias causes us to seek out information that confirms our preexisting beliefs while disregarding or downplaying any contradictory evidence. It is a natural tendency to want to feel validated in our opinions, but this bias can prevent us from considering alternative perspectives and hinder our ability to make informed decisions.

Another prevalent bias is the availability heuristic, which is the tendency to rely on readily available information when making judgments or decisions. Our minds often rely on the ease with which examples or instances come to mind, leading us to overestimate the likelihood or importance of certain events. This bias can lead to poor decision-making, as it may cause us to overlook less obvious but more relevant information.

The anchoring bias is another cognitive bias that influences decision-making. This bias occurs when we rely too heavily on the first piece of information we encounter when evaluating options. This initial reference point, or "anchor," can influence subsequent judgments, causing us to make decisions based on a skewed perception.

Understanding these biases and their potential effects on our decision-making processes is the first step towards overcoming them. By actively acknowledging and questioning our own biases, we can strive for more objective and rational decision-making.

To combat confirmation bias, it is essential to actively seek out diverse viewpoints and consider alternative perspectives. Engaging in open-minded discussions or seeking out information that challenges our beliefs can help us make more well-rounded decisions.

Overcoming the availability heuristic requires consciously seeking out additional information and considering the potential biases or limitations of the examples that readily come to mind. By actively searching for more comprehensive and balanced information, we can make better-informed decisions.

To counteract the anchoring bias, it is helpful to explore a range of options before settling on a decision. By considering multiple reference points and deliberately seeking out different perspectives, we can avoid fixating on a single anchor and make more unbiased choices.

Recognizing and understanding these cognitive biases is crucial in improving decision-making skills. By actively challenging our biases and seeking out diverse perspectives and information, we can empower ourselves to make more informed and rational choices. The power of choice lies in our ability to overcome these biases and make decisions that align with our true values and goals.

Emotional Factors in Decision-Making

Emotions play a significant role in our decision-making process. Whether we realize it or not, our emotions can heavily influence the choices we make. In this subchapter, we will explore the various emotional factors that impact decision-making and how we can effectively navigate them.

One crucial emotional factor is fear. Fear can either paralyze us or push us to make hasty decisions. When faced with a potentially risky decision, fear can cloud our judgment and prevent us from objectively considering all the available options. Recognizing and acknowledging our fears is essential in order to make rational decisions. By examining the source of our fear and evaluating the potential consequences, we can overcome it and make more informed choices.

Another emotional factor is excitement. Excitement can lead us to make impulsive decisions without thoroughly evaluating the long-term effects. It is important to channel our excitement into rational thinking by taking a step back and considering all the potential outcomes. By balancing our emotions with logical reasoning, we can ensure that our decisions are based on sound judgment rather than temporary excitement.

Additionally, happiness can greatly impact our decision-making process. When we are in a positive state of mind, we tend to be more optimistic and less risk-averse. This can lead us to overlook potential pitfalls and make decisions based solely on short-term gratification. It is crucial to maintain a balanced perspective and consider both the immediate benefits and long-term consequences of our choices.

On the other hand, sadness and disappointment can also heavily influence our decision-making. When we are feeling down, we may be more inclined to make impulsive decisions as a way to escape or distract ourselves from our negative emotions. It is important to recognize these tendencies and practice self-awareness when making decisions during difficult times. Seeking support from loved ones or professionals can also provide valuable guidance during these emotionally challenging periods.

In conclusion, emotions have a profound impact on our decision-making process. By understanding and addressing the emotional factors that influence our choices, we can make more informed and balanced decisions. It is essential to be self-aware, analyze our emotions, and ensure that our decision-making process is grounded in rational thinking. By doing so, we can harness the power of our emotions to empower our decision-making and create a more fulfilling and successful life.

Social Influences on Decision-Making

In today's interconnected world, social influences play a crucial role in shaping our decision-making process. Whether we are aware of it or not, the opinions, attitudes, and actions of others can significantly impact the choices we make in our lives. Understanding these social influences is essential if we want to make informed decisions that align with our values and aspirations. This subchapter explores the various ways in which social factors can influence our decision-making and offers strategies to empower everyone in their decision-making process.

One significant social influence on decision-making is peer pressure. From a young age, we learn to conform to the norms and expectations of our social groups. This desire to fit in can often cloud our judgment and lead us to make choices that may not be in our best interest. By recognizing the influence of peer pressure, we can start to make decisions that truly reflect our own desires and beliefs.

Another powerful social influence is the media. Through television, movies, social media, and advertising, we are constantly bombarded with images and messages that shape our perceptions of what is desirable or acceptable. It is crucial to develop media literacy skills to critically analyze these influences and make decisions based on our own values rather than blindly following societal trends.

Furthermore, family and cultural backgrounds also play a significant role in decision-making. Our upbringing and the values instilled in us by our families and communities can heavily influence the choices we make. However, it is essential to recognize that our decisions should not solely be based on tradition or societal expectations. We must strive to make decisions that align with our personal goals and aspirations, even if they may diverge from our cultural norms.

To empower everyone in their decision-making, it is crucial to develop self-awareness and a strong sense of personal identity. By understanding our own values, strengths, and weaknesses, we can make decisions that are authentic and true to ourselves. Additionally, seeking diverse perspectives and engaging in open-minded discussions can help us gain new insights and challenge our own biases.

Ultimately, the power of choice lies in our hands. By recognizing and understanding the social influences on decision-making, we can take control of our own lives and make decisions that will lead us towards a more fulfilling future. This subchapter aims to equip everyone with the tools and knowledge needed to navigate the complex web of social influences and make decisions that align with their own unique journey.

Chapter 3: Enhancing Decision-Making Skills

Self-Awareness and Decision-Making

In the vast landscape of decision-making, self-awareness acts as a compass, guiding us towards choices that align with our values, goals, and aspirations. The ability to understand ourselves on a deeper level is the cornerstone of effective decision-making. In this subchapter, we will explore the crucial role of self-awareness in the decision-making process and delve into strategies that empower everyone to make informed choices.

Self-awareness begins with introspection – the conscious examination of our thoughts, emotions, and beliefs. By taking the time to understand our own motivations and biases, we can navigate the decision-making process with clarity and authenticity. This awareness enables us to recognize our strengths, weaknesses, and values, providing a solid foundation from which to make decisions that resonate with our true selves.

One powerful tool for cultivating self-awareness is mindfulness. By practicing mindfulness, we can observe our thoughts and emotions without judgment, allowing us to gain insight into our decision-making patterns. Mindfulness teaches us to pause and reflect before making choices, ensuring that our decisions are not driven by impulsive reactions or external pressures.

Another essential aspect of self-awareness is understanding our personal values. When we are aware of what truly matters to us, we can align our decisions with our core principles. Reflecting on our values helps us prioritize our goals and make choices that are in harmony with our long-term vision.

Moreover, self-awareness helps us recognize our decision-making biases. We all have inherent cognitive biases that can cloud our judgment. By acknowledging these biases, such as confirmation bias or the tendency to seek information that confirms our pre-existing beliefs, we can challenge them and make more objective choices.

Developing self-awareness also involves assessing our emotions. Emotions play a significant role in decision-making, often influencing our choices. By understanding and managing our emotions, we can prevent them from clouding our judgment. Emotional intelligence, the ability to recognize and regulate emotions, enhances our decision-making by providing a balanced perspective.

In conclusion, self-awareness is an invaluable asset in the decision-making process. By cultivating self-awareness through introspection, mindfulness, understanding personal values, recognizing biases, and managing emotions, we empower ourselves to make choices that align with our authentic selves. Harnessing the power of self-awareness enables everyone to approach decision-making with clarity, confidence, and integrity. By making conscious choices, we can shape our lives and navigate the complexities of decision-making with grace and wisdom.

Critical Thinking for Better Decisions

Subchapter: Critical Thinking for Better Decisions

Introduction:
In today's fast-paced world, making decisions has become an integral part of our daily lives. Whether it is choosing a career path, making financial investments, or even deciding what to have for dinner, the choices we make shape our future. However, many of us struggle with making effective decisions that align with our goals and values. This subchapter aims to empower every individual with the tools and techniques of critical thinking to enhance their decision-making skills.

Understanding   Critical   Thinking:
Critical thinking is an essential skill that enables us to objectively analyze information, evaluate options, and make well-informed decisions. It involves questioning assumptions, examining evidence, and considering different perspectives before arriving at a conclusion. By cultivating critical thinking, we can overcome biases, make logical connections, and arrive at better decisions.

The   Key   Elements   of   Critical   Thinking:
1. Analysis: Critical thinking starts with gathering relevant information and breaking it down into manageable parts. By examining the facts, data, and evidence available, we can identify patterns, trends, and potential outcomes.

2. Evaluation: Once we have analyzed the information, it is crucial to evaluate its reliability, credibility, and relevance. By questioning the source, considering alternative viewpoints, and weighing the pros and cons, we can make more informed choices.

3. Problem-solving: Critical thinking helps us identify and define problems accurately. By using logical reasoning and creativity, we can generate and evaluate potential solutions, considering both short-term and long-term consequences.

4. Decision-making: After evaluating the available options, critical thinking allows us to make decisions that align with our goals, values, and priorities. It helps us anticipate potential risks, consider the impact on others, and choose the best course of action.

Benefits of Critical Thinking:
1. Enhanced problem-solving skills: Critical thinking enables us to think outside the box, explore innovative solutions, and overcome challenges effectively.

2. Improved decision-making: By utilizing critical thinking, we can make decisions based on evidence and logic rather than emotions or biases, leading to better outcomes.

3. Reduced risks and errors: Critical thinking helps us anticipate potential risks and avoid hasty decisions, minimizing the chances of making costly mistakes.

4. Increased self-awareness: By engaging in critical thinking, we become more aware of our own biases, assumptions, and limitations, allowing us to make decisions that align with our authentic selves.

Conclusion:
In the realm of decision-making, critical thinking serves as a powerful tool to navigate the complexities of life. By honing this skill, we can make better choices, achieve our goals, and lead a more fulfilling life.

Embracing critical thinking enables us to approach decision-making with clarity, objectivity, and confidence, empowering us to take charge of our destiny. So, let us embark on this journey of critical thinking and unlock the power of choice.

Analyzing Risks and Rewards

Making decisions is an integral part of our daily lives. Whether we are choosing what to eat for breakfast or deciding on a career path, each decision we make carries a certain level of risk and reward. Understanding how to analyze these risks and rewards is crucial to making informed and empowered choices. In this subchapter, we will explore the principles behind analyzing risks and rewards and how they can guide us towards better decision-making.

To begin, it is important to recognize that every decision we make involves some level of uncertainty. Risks are the potential negative outcomes or consequences associated with a particular choice. Rewards, on the other hand, are the benefits or positive outcomes that we hope to achieve. By assessing both the risks and rewards, we can gain a clearer understanding of the potential outcomes of our decisions.

One key aspect of analyzing risks and rewards is evaluating the probability of each outcome. This involves gathering relevant information, examining past experiences, and considering expert opinions. By assessing the likelihood of different outcomes, we can prioritize our choices and make more calculated decisions.

Furthermore, it is essential to consider the magnitude of each risk and reward. Some outcomes may have a significant impact on our lives, while others may be relatively minor. By weighing the potential consequences, we can determine the level of risk we are willing to accept. Similarly, understanding the potential rewards can help us identify opportunities for growth and success.

In addition to evaluating risks and rewards, it is crucial to consider our own values, preferences, and goals. What may be a significant risk for one person may be an acceptable level for another. By aligning our decisions with our personal values and aspirations, we can make choices that are truly meaningful and fulfilling.

Finally, it is important to remember that analyzing risks and rewards is an ongoing process. As circumstances change and new information becomes available, we must be willing to reassess our decisions and adjust our strategies accordingly. By continuously evaluating and learning from our choices, we can navigate through life with confidence and resilience.

In conclusion, analyzing risks and rewards is a fundamental skill in making informed decisions. By assessing the probability and magnitude of potential outcomes, considering our values and goals, and embracing the dynamic nature of decision-making, we can empower ourselves to make choices that align with our desires and lead to a more fulfilling life.

Chapter 4: Overcoming Decision-Making Challenges

Decision Paralysis and Procrastination

In today's fast-paced world, making decisions has become an integral part of our lives. From choosing what to wear in the morning to making life-altering decisions, the ability to make choices is something we all possess. However, many of us often find ourselves stuck in a state of indecision, unable to move forward or make progress. This phenomenon is commonly known as decision paralysis and procrastination.

Decision paralysis occurs when we are presented with too many options or when the consequences of our choices seem overwhelming. The fear of making the wrong decision often leads us to a state of analysis paralysis, where we endlessly weigh the pros and cons without reaching a conclusion. This indecisiveness can lead to missed opportunities, increased stress, and a lack of direction in life.

Procrastination, on the other hand, is the act of delaying or postponing making a decision. It is a psychological defense mechanism that often stems from fear or anxiety. We may put off making a decision because we are afraid of the potential outcomes or uncertain about the future. However, this only prolongs the process and increases our anxiety levels.

So how can we overcome decision paralysis and procrastination? The first step is to recognize and acknowledge that we are stuck in this pattern. Awareness is key to initiating change. Once we are aware of our tendency to procrastinate or get trapped in decision paralysis, we can take action to break free from it.

One effective technique is to set clear goals and priorities. By identifying what truly matters to us and what we want to achieve, we can eliminate unnecessary choices and focus on what is truly important. This clarity helps us make decisions more efficiently and with greater confidence.

Another strategy is to gather information and seek advice from trusted sources. Sometimes, the fear of making the wrong decision stems from a lack of knowledge or understanding. By conducting thorough research and consulting experts or mentors, we can gain valuable insights and make more informed choices.

Additionally, it is crucial to trust our instincts and listen to our intuition. Often, our gut feelings provide valuable guidance that can help us make decisions more effectively. Learning to trust ourselves and our intuition can be a powerful tool in overcoming decision paralysis and procrastination.

In conclusion, decision paralysis and procrastination can hinder our progress and limit our potential. However, by recognizing these patterns and implementing strategies to overcome them, we can empower ourselves to make better decisions. With clear goals, informed choices, and trust in our instincts, we can break free from indecision and take control of our lives. The power of choice lies within each and every one of us, waiting to be unleashed.

Dealing with Uncertainty and Ambiguity

In the realm of decision-making, uncertainty and ambiguity are two formidable adversaries that can often leave us feeling stuck or overwhelmed. However, it is important to recognize that they are an inevitable part of life, and learning how to navigate through them can greatly empower our decision-making abilities. This subchapter aims to equip you with the necessary tools and mindset to effectively deal with uncertainty and ambiguity, enabling you to make confident and informed choices.

Uncertainty arises when we lack complete knowledge or information about a situation, outcome, or potential consequences. It can be daunting, as it leaves us with a sense of doubt and insecurity. However, embracing uncertainty as an opportunity for growth is crucial. Instead of fearing the unknown, view it as a chance to explore new possibilities and expand your perspective. Recognize that it is impossible to have all the answers, and that making decisions in the face of uncertainty is a testament to your courage and resilience.

Ambiguity, on the other hand, refers to situations where multiple interpretations or meanings are possible. It can be particularly challenging because it requires us to navigate through a maze of possibilities, often without clear guidelines. To effectively deal with ambiguity, cultivate your ability to tolerate discomfort and seek clarity. Break down complex situations into smaller, more manageable parts, and approach them with an open mind. Engage in active listening and ask questions to gain a deeper understanding of the different perspectives at play. By embracing ambiguity, you open yourself up to diverse viewpoints and increase the chances of making well-rounded decisions.

In addition to these strategies, cultivating a mindset of adaptability and flexibility is crucial when dealing with uncertainty and ambiguity. Recognize that decision-making is not a linear process, and sometimes adjustments and course corrections are necessary. Embrace the idea that mistakes or failures are not the end but rather stepping stones to success. Learn from your experiences, and use them to refine your decision-making skills.

Remember, everyone faces uncertainty and ambiguity at various points in their lives. By acknowledging these challenges and developing effective strategies to navigate through them, you empower yourself to make decisions with confidence and clarity. Embrace uncertainty as an opportunity for growth, and approach ambiguity with curiosity and an open mind. With these tools in hand, you are well-equipped to harness the power of choice and make decisions that align with your values and goals.

Managing Regret and Post-Decision Dissonance

Regret is an emotion that all of us have experienced at some point in our lives. It is that feeling of disappointment or dissatisfaction with a decision we have made. Whether it is a small decision like choosing what to wear or a major life-altering decision, regret can creep in and leave us feeling uneasy. However, it is important to remember that regret is a natural part of the decision-making process and can offer valuable lessons for the future.

One of the key aspects of managing regret is understanding that we are only human and prone to making mistakes. We must accept that not every decision will lead to the desired outcome, but that does not mean we should beat ourselves up over it. Instead, we should focus on learning from our mistakes and using them as stepping stones towards better decision-making in the future.

Post-decision dissonance is another phenomenon closely related to regret. It refers to the discomfort or unease we feel after making a decision, especially when there are conflicting options or alternatives. This dissonance arises from the fear of missing out on what could have been if we had chosen differently. To manage post-decision dissonance, it is crucial to remind ourselves of the reasons why we made the decision in the first place. We need to trust our judgment and have confidence in our ability to make sound choices.

One effective strategy for managing regret and post-decision dissonance is to engage in proactive reflection. Take the time to evaluate your decisions, both good and bad, and identify the factors that influenced your choices. This reflection will enable you to gain a better understanding of your decision-making patterns and make adjustments accordingly. It may also help you identify any biases or external pressures that may have affected your judgment.

Additionally, seeking support from others can be incredibly helpful in managing regret and post-decision dissonance. Discussing your decisions with trusted friends, family, or mentors can provide you with different perspectives and insights that you may have overlooked. They can also offer encouragement and reassurance, helping you navigate through feelings of regret.

In conclusion, managing regret and post-decision dissonance is an essential skill in the realm of decision-making. By accepting our fallibility, engaging in proactive reflection, and seeking support, we can effectively navigate through these emotions and use them as tools for growth and self-improvement. Remember, every decision is an opportunity to learn and make better choices in the future.

Chapter 5: Decision-Making in Relationships

Collaborative Decision-Making

In today's complex and interconnected world, the ability to make effective decisions is paramount. We are constantly faced with choices that can have a profound impact on our personal and professional lives. However, making decisions in isolation can be overwhelming and often leads to suboptimal outcomes. That's where collaborative decision-making comes into play.

Collaborative decision-making is a process that involves gathering input and perspectives from a diverse group of individuals to reach a consensus or make a collective choice. It harnesses the power of collective intelligence, enabling us to tap into the wisdom of the crowd and make more informed and balanced decisions.

One of the key benefits of collaborative decision-making is the opportunity to bring together different perspectives and expertise. When we work collaboratively, we can leverage the unique knowledge and skills of each team member, enhancing the quality of our decisions. By considering multiple viewpoints, we can identify blind spots, uncover hidden risks, and evaluate potential alternatives more thoroughly.

Moreover, collaborative decision-making fosters a sense of ownership and accountability among participants. When individuals are actively involved in the decision-making process, they are more likely to support and implement the chosen course of action. This not only improves the overall effectiveness of the decision but also enhances team cohesion and morale.

To facilitate collaborative decision-making, it is crucial to establish a culture of trust and open communication. Participants should feel comfortable expressing their opinions, challenging assumptions, and engaging in constructive debates. Active listening and empathy play a vital role in creating an inclusive environment where everyone's voice is heard and respected.

In addition, technology can be a valuable tool for collaborative decision-making. Online platforms and virtual collaboration tools enable geographically dispersed teams to collaborate in real-time, overcoming the limitations of physical distance. These tools also provide a centralized space for sharing information, capturing ideas, and documenting the decision-making process.

However, it is important to note that collaborative decision-making is not without its challenges. It requires time, resources, and a commitment to the process. Conflicting opinions, power dynamics, and a fear of change can also hinder effective collaboration. Therefore, it is essential to establish clear roles, norms, and decision-making protocols to navigate these challenges successfully.

Ultimately, collaborative decision-making empowers individuals and teams to make better choices by harnessing the collective knowledge and expertise. By embracing a collaborative approach, we can tap into the power of choice and unlock the full potential of our decision-making capabilities. Whether in our personal lives or professional endeavors, collaborative decision-making offers a pathway to better outcomes, increased innovation, and a stronger sense of community.

Resolving Conflicts through Effective Decision-Making

Conflicts are an inevitable part of life. Whether it's a disagreement with a colleague, a family member, or a friend, conflicts can arise in various situations. However, what sets individuals apart is their ability to resolve these conflicts through effective decision-making. In this subchapter, we will delve into the power of choice and how it empowers everyone to resolve conflicts successfully.

The key to resolving conflicts lies in making sound decisions. Decision-making is a skill that can be honed and refined, enabling individuals to navigate through challenging situations with grace and clarity. It involves critically analyzing the options available and choosing the one that aligns with one's values, goals, and priorities. By harnessing the power of choice, individuals can proactively address conflicts and arrive at mutually satisfactory solutions.

One of the essential aspects of effective decision-making is maintaining a rational mindset. Emotions often run high during conflicts, clouding judgment and hindering the decision-making process. It is crucial to step back, take a deep breath, and approach the situation with a calm and rational mindset. By doing so, individuals can evaluate the conflict objectively, separate facts from emotions, and make decisions that are in the best interest of all parties involved.

Furthermore, effective decision-making requires active listening and empathetic understanding. Conflicts often arise due to differing perspectives and misunderstandings. By actively listening to all parties involved and seeking to understand their viewpoints, individuals can gain valuable insights and find common ground. This empathetic approach fosters open communication, encourages collaboration, and paves the way for win-win solutions.

Another vital aspect of resolving conflicts through effective decision-making is considering the long-term consequences. It's easy to get caught up in the heat of the moment and make impulsive decisions that may have negative repercussions in the future. By carefully weighing the potential outcomes and considering the long-term implications, individuals can make decisions that not only resolve the immediate conflict but also promote harmony and growth in the long run.

In conclusion, resolving conflicts through effective decision-making is a powerful tool that empowers everyone. By embracing the power of choice, maintaining a rational mindset, actively listening, and considering long-term consequences, individuals can navigate conflicts with confidence and grace. This subchapter serves as a guide for anyone seeking to enhance their decision-making skills in order to resolve conflicts and foster healthy relationships. Remember, the choice is yours – choose wisely, and resolve conflicts effectively.

Supporting Others in their Decision-Making Processes

Making decisions is an integral part of our everyday lives. Whether it's choosing what to wear, where to go for lunch, or making major life-changing decisions, we are constantly faced with choices. However, decision-making can often be a daunting and overwhelming process, leaving us feeling unsure and uncertain. In such times, it is crucial to have a support system in place that can guide and empower us in making the best decisions for ourselves.

Supporting others in their decision-making processes is not only a noble gesture, but it also promotes growth and self-confidence. By lending a helping hand, we can assist individuals in navigating through the complexities of decision-making, allowing them to feel empowered and capable of making choices that align with their desires and values.

One of the most important aspects of supporting others in their decision-making is active listening. Being fully present and engaged in the conversation enables us to understand the individual's concerns, fears, and goals. By empathetically listening, we allow them to express their thoughts and emotions freely, providing a safe space for exploration and self-reflection.

Another key element in supporting others is offering unbiased advice. It is crucial to provide a non-judgmental perspective that encourages critical thinking and self-discovery. Instead of imposing our own opinions, we should encourage individuals to explore various options, weigh the pros and cons, and consider the potential outcomes of each choice. This approach allows for a more holistic decision-making process, where individuals can identify their own values and priorities.

Furthermore, it is important to remind individuals that making mistakes is a natural part of the decision-making process. Encourage them to view setbacks as opportunities for growth and learning rather than failures. By fostering a supportive environment that embraces trial and error, individuals can gain confidence in their decision-making abilities and develop resilience for future challenges.

Lastly, celebrating successes, no matter how big or small, is vital in supporting others. Acknowledging and validating their efforts reinforces their confidence and reinforces the belief in their decision-making skills. By celebrating achievements, we create a positive feedback loop that encourages individuals to continue making choices that align with their values and aspirations.

In conclusion, supporting others in their decision-making processes is an essential act of empowerment and growth. By actively listening, offering unbiased advice, embracing mistakes, and celebrating successes, we can create a nurturing environment that encourages individuals to make choices that align with their values. Remember, we all have the power to make decisions that shape our lives, and by supporting one another, we can collectively navigate the vast landscape of decision-making with confidence and clarity.

Chapter 6: Decision-Making in Professional Life

Decision-Making in the Workplace

Introduction:
In today's fast-paced and dynamic work environment, the ability to make effective decisions is crucial for success. Whether you are a manager, an employee, or an entrepreneur, your ability to make sound choices can significantly impact your career trajectory and the overall success of your organization. This subchapter titled "Decision-Making in the Workplace" aims to explore the various aspects of decision-making and provide valuable insights to empower everyone in making better choices.

Understanding the Decision-Making Process:
The decision-making process involves several steps that help individuals and teams come to a conclusion. From identifying the problem or opportunity to evaluating alternatives and selecting the best course of action, each step plays a vital role. This subchapter will delve into each stage, offering practical tips and techniques to improve your decision-making skills.

Factors Influencing Decision-Making:
Numerous factors can influence our decision-making abilities in the workplace. These may include personal biases, time constraints, limited information, and the pressure to make quick decisions. By understanding these factors, we can better navigate through them and make more informed choices. This subchapter will address these influences and provide strategies to mitigate their impact on decision-making.

Collaborative   Decision-Making:
In many workplaces, decisions are not made in isolation but rather involve collaboration with colleagues or team members. Collaborative decision-making can harness the collective wisdom and diverse perspectives of a group, leading to better outcomes. This subchapter will explore the benefits of collaborative decision-making, outline effective communication strategies, and highlight the importance of fostering a culture that values collaboration.

Ethical   Decision-Making:
Making ethical decisions in the workplace is essential to maintain integrity and trust. It is crucial to navigate ethical dilemmas with a strong moral compass and an understanding of the potential consequences. This subchapter will explore ethical decision-making frameworks, such as utilitarianism and deontological ethics, to guide individuals in making morally responsible choices.

Embracing   Failure   and   Learning   from   Mistakes:
In the workplace, not all decisions yield the desired outcomes. Embracing failure as an opportunity for growth and learning is essential for personal and professional development. This subchapter will emphasize the importance of resilience, providing strategies to bounce back from failure and leverage it as a stepping stone towards success.

Conclusion:
Effective decision-making is a vital skill that can be honed and developed over time. By understanding and applying the principles discussed in this subchapter, individuals from all walks of life can enhance their decision-making abilities in the workplace. Whether

you are a seasoned professional or just starting your career, the power of choice lies in your hands. Empower yourself to make informed decisions, and watch your personal and professional life flourish.

Ethical Decision-Making

In a world full of choices, it becomes increasingly important to make decisions that not only benefit ourselves but also align with our moral compass. Ethical decision-making is the process of evaluating the potential consequences of our choices on both ourselves and others, and choosing the course of action that upholds our values and principles.

The Power of Choice: Empowering Everyone's Decision-Making explores the significance of ethical decision-making in our daily lives. Whether it's choosing between right and wrong, good and bad, or prioritizing the needs of others over our own, ethical decision-making plays a vital role in shaping our character and the world around us.

Making decisions is an inherent part of being human. From simple choices like what to eat for breakfast to complex decisions that impact our careers, relationships, and society, our choices shape our lives. However, the quality of our decisions should not only be measured by their outcomes but also by the ethical considerations behind them.

Ethical decision-making requires us to consider the potential consequences of our choices on others. It urges us to think beyond our immediate interests and consider the greater good. By embracing ethics in decision-making, we can build a society that values empathy, fairness, and justice.

In this subchapter, we delve into the principles and frameworks that guide ethical decision-making. We explore the role of empathy, moral reasoning, and the importance of considering different perspectives.

By understanding these core concepts, we can navigate the complexities of decision-making with greater clarity and integrity.

Furthermore, we address the challenges that arise when making ethical decisions. Sometimes, doing the right thing may conflict with personal gain or societal pressures. We explore strategies for overcoming these hurdles and staying true to our ethical principles.

Finally, we highlight real-life examples of ethical decision-making to inspire and educate readers. By examining case studies from various fields, we demonstrate how individuals have made choices that prioritize ethics, even in the face of adversity.

Ethical decision-making is not just a philosophical concept; it is a practical tool for living a purposeful and responsible life. The Power of Choice: Empowering Everyone's Decision-Making equips readers with the knowledge and skills to make ethical decisions that positively impact their lives and the world around them. By embracing ethical decision-making, we can create a society in which every choice becomes an opportunity to make a difference.

Leadership and Decision-Making

In the journey of life, we are constantly faced with decisions both big and small. From choosing what to have for breakfast to making life-altering career choices, decision-making plays a crucial role in shaping our future. However, the ability to make effective decisions is not something that comes naturally to everyone. It requires leadership skills to navigate through the complexities and uncertainties that decision-making presents.

Leadership and decision-making are intrinsically linked. A true leader possesses the ability to make sound judgments, analyze situations, and inspire others to follow their lead. They understand the importance of making informed decisions that align with their values, goals, and the greater good. By mastering the art of decision-making, anyone can become a leader in their own right.

In this subchapter, "Leadership and Decision-Making," we will explore the fundamental principles of leadership and how they intersect with the decision-making process. We will delve into the qualities that define a successful leader and the impact their decisions have on both themselves and those around them. By understanding these concepts, we can empower ourselves to make better choices and lead others towards a brighter future.

One key aspect of leadership is the ability to gather and analyze information. Leaders understand the importance of seeking diverse perspectives and considering all available options before making a decision. They know that rushing into a choice without proper evaluation can lead to undesirable outcomes. By adopting a systematic approach to decision-making, we can ensure that our choices are well-informed and have a higher chance of success.

Furthermore, effective leaders possess strong communication skills. They are able to articulate their vision, inspire others, and foster collaboration. By fostering open and transparent communication, leaders can create an environment where everyone feels valued and empowered to contribute their ideas. This inclusive approach to decision-making not only leads to better choices but also promotes a sense of ownership and commitment among team members.

Lastly, this subchapter will explore the concept of ethical decision-making. True leaders understand the importance of making decisions that align with their values and principles. They consider the impact of their choices on others and strive to make decisions that are fair, just, and ethical. By incorporating ethical considerations into our decision-making process, we can build trust, integrity, and credibility as leaders.

In conclusion, leadership and decision-making go hand in hand. By developing leadership skills and embracing a systematic approach to decision-making, we can become effective leaders in our own lives. This subchapter will equip you with the knowledge and tools to make informed choices, inspire others, and create a positive impact. Remember, each decision you make has the power to shape your future and the world around you. Embrace the power of choice and embark on a journey towards empowered decision-making and leadership.

Chapter 7: The Power of Intuition in Decision-Making

Developing Intuition as a Decision-Making Tool

In our fast-paced and complex world, making decisions has become an integral part of our daily lives. Whether it's deciding on a career path, choosing a life partner, or even making small everyday choices, the ability to make effective decisions is crucial. However, with so many options and variables to consider, decision-making can often feel overwhelming and daunting.

One powerful tool that we all possess but often fail to utilize to its full potential is our intuition. Intuition is that gut feeling or inner knowing that guides us without conscious reasoning. It is an innate ability that we can tap into to make better decisions and navigate through life's challenges.

Developing intuition as a decision-making tool requires self-awareness and trust in oneself. To begin, it is important to cultivate a quiet mind through practices such as meditation or mindfulness. These practices help us to calm the noise and chatter in our minds, allowing our intuition to come to the forefront. By creating space for reflection and introspection, we can become more attuned to our inner wisdom.

Listening to our intuition involves paying attention to our emotions and sensations. Our bodies often give us subtle cues that can guide us towards the right decision. A feeling of lightness or expansiveness may indicate that a choice is aligned with our true selves, while a sense of heaviness or contraction may signal that it is not. By honing in on these intuitive signals, we can gain valuable insights into the decisions we face.

However, developing intuition does not mean disregarding rationality or logic. Intuition and reason can work in harmony to enhance our decision-making abilities. It is important to gather all relevant information, analyze the pros and cons, and consider the potential consequences of our choices. Once we have weighed the rational aspects, we can then consult our intuition for a final decision.

Practicing intuition as a decision-making tool may require stepping out of our comfort zones and taking risks. It involves trusting ourselves and being open to the unknown. However, as we continue to hone this skill, we will find that our intuition becomes a reliable compass, guiding us towards choices that align with our values and aspirations.

In conclusion, developing intuition as a decision-making tool can empower us to navigate life's complexities with greater ease and confidence. By cultivating self-awareness, listening to our emotions, and integrating intuition with reason, we can tap into our inner wisdom and make choices that are in alignment with our true selves. So, let us embrace our intuition, and unlock the power of choice within us.

Trusting Your Gut: Intuition vs. Analysis

In the realm of decision-making, we often find ourselves caught between two powerful forces: intuition and analysis. While some swear by the power of their gut feelings, others rely solely on logical thinking and rational analysis. But what if we told you that both intuition and analysis have their merits and can be harnessed to make better choices?

Intuition, often referred to as a gut feeling or instinct, is our ability to make quick decisions based on our subconscious knowledge and experiences. It is that little voice inside us that whispers a warning or encourages us to take a leap of faith. Intuition is a powerful tool, honed through years of experience and exposure to various situations. It allows us to tap into our inner wisdom and make decisions that may seem illogical at first glance but prove to be right in the long run.

On the other hand, analysis is a logical and systematic approach to decision-making. It involves gathering data, conducting research, and carefully considering all the pros and cons before reaching a conclusion. Analysis helps us evaluate risks, calculate potential outcomes, and make informed choices based on facts and evidence. It is the embodiment of rationality and can help us avoid impulsive decisions or unnecessary risks.

But how do we strike the right balance between intuition and analysis? The key lies in understanding that they are not mutually exclusive but complementary forces. By combining both intuition and analysis, we can make decisions that are both informed and aligned with our deeper sense of knowing.

When faced with a decision, start by gathering all the relevant information and conducting a thorough analysis. Consider the facts, weigh the pros and cons, and evaluate the potential outcomes. This analytical process will provide you with a solid foundation to base your decision upon. However, don't stop there. Take a moment to tune in to your intuition. What does your gut feeling tell you? Does it align with the logical analysis or offer a different perspective? Trust your intuition, but also question and explore it further.

Remember that intuition is not infallible, just as analysis is not foolproof. It is essential to validate your gut feeling with logical reasoning and evidence. By doing so, you can make decisions that are not only guided by your inner wisdom but also supported by a logical framework.

In conclusion, the power of choice lies in harnessing both intuition and analysis. By trusting your gut while also engaging in a thorough analysis, you can make decisions that are truly empowering. So, embrace the duality of intuition and analysis, and unlock the full potential of your decision-making abilities.

Combining Intuition and Rational Thinking

In the realm of decision-making, there are two powerful tools at our disposal: intuition and rational thinking. While these approaches may seem contradictory, they actually complement each other in a remarkable way, leading to more effective and fulfilling decision-making. In this subchapter, we explore the art of combining intuition and rational thinking to empower everyone's decision-making process.

Intuition, often referred to as our "gut feeling," is a powerful inner voice that guides us without conscious reasoning. It is a subconscious process that draws on our past experiences, knowledge, and emotions, allowing us to make quick decisions based on our instincts. On the other hand, rational thinking relies on logical analysis, evidence, and facts to reach a well-reasoned conclusion. By combining these two approaches, we can tap into a more holistic decision-making process.

Intuition plays a significant role in decision-making by providing us with valuable insights that our rational mind may overlook. It can help us recognize patterns, identify opportunities, and sense potential risks. By listening to our intuition, we can access our inner wisdom and make decisions that align with our authentic selves. However, intuition alone can sometimes be clouded by biases, emotions, or limited perspectives, which is where rational thinking comes into play.

Rational thinking acts as a balancing force to ensure that our decisions are grounded in logic and evidence. By analyzing the pros and cons, considering various alternatives, and gathering relevant information, we can make more objective and informed choices. Rational thinking helps us evaluate the potential outcomes, identify potential pitfalls, and weigh the consequences of our decisions. It encourages us to question assumptions, challenge biases, and think critically.

The key to harnessing the power of combining intuition and rational thinking lies in finding a balance between the two. It is important to listen to our intuitive insights and trust our instincts, but also to subject them to rational scrutiny. By critically examining our intuitive feelings and subjecting them to logical analysis, we can gain a deeper understanding of our choices and make more well-rounded decisions.

In conclusion, the art of combining intuition and rational thinking is a crucial skill in the realm of decision-making. By honoring our intuitive insights and subjecting them to rational analysis, we can tap into a more holistic approach that empowers us to make effective and fulfilling choices. So, next time you are faced with a decision, embrace both your intuition and rational thinking, and unlock the power of choice.

Chapter 8: Applying Decision-Making Principles in Everyday Life

Making Better Financial Decisions

In today's fast-paced world, where money plays a significant role in our lives, making sound financial decisions is crucial. Whether you are a young adult just starting your career or a seasoned professional planning for retirement, understanding how to make better financial choices can have a profound impact on your financial well-being. This subchapter aims to empower everyone with the knowledge and tools necessary to make informed financial decisions.

The first step in making better financial decisions is to educate yourself about personal finance. Many individuals lack a basic understanding of financial concepts, such as budgeting, saving, and investing. By familiarizing yourself with these principles, you can develop a solid foundation for making informed choices.

Budgeting is a fundamental aspect of personal finance. It allows you to track your income and expenses and ensure that you live within your means. Creating a budget helps you prioritize your spending, save for future goals, and avoid unnecessary debt.

Saving is another critical aspect of financial decision-making. It is essential to set aside a portion of your income for emergencies and future goals, such as buying a house or funding your children's education. By cultivating the habit of saving, you can build a financial safety net and achieve long-term financial stability.

Investing is an effective way to grow your wealth over time. However, it is essential to understand the risks and potential rewards associated with different investment options. Educate yourself about various investment vehicles, such as stocks, bonds, and mutual funds, and consider seeking professional advice to make informed investment decisions.

Avoiding impulsive purchases and practicing delayed gratification is also crucial for making better financial choices. Before making significant purchases, take the time to evaluate whether it aligns with your long-term financial goals. Impulsive buying can undermine your financial health and hinder your ability to achieve financial freedom.

In conclusion, making better financial decisions is a skill that everyone should develop. By understanding personal finance principles, budgeting, saving, investing wisely, and practicing delayed gratification, you can take control of your financial future. Empower yourself with the knowledge and tools necessary to make sound financial choices, and pave the way to a more prosperous and secure future.

Health-Related Decision-Making

In our journey through life, we are faced with countless decisions. Some decisions are trivial, like what to wear or what to have for breakfast. However, there are decisions that hold far greater significance, particularly those related to our health. These decisions can have a profound impact on our overall well-being and quality of life.

Health-related decision-making is a critical aspect of our lives that we all encounter at some point, regardless of age or background. From choosing a healthcare provider to deciding on a treatment plan, these decisions shape our physical and mental health outcomes. Therefore, it is essential to empower ourselves with the knowledge and skills necessary to make informed and effective choices.

One of the key factors in making health-related decisions is understanding the available options. This requires gathering relevant information, consulting professionals, and seeking out credible sources. By taking an active role in our healthcare, we can make decisions that align with our values, preferences, and goals.

Another crucial aspect of health-related decision-making is considering the potential risks and benefits of each option. Weighing the pros and cons allows us to make choices that maximize our well-being while minimizing potential harm. Additionally, considering the long-term implications of our decisions can help us make choices that promote sustainable health and prevent future issues.

Emotional factors also play a significant role in health-related decision-making. Fear, anxiety, and uncertainty can cloud our judgment and hinder our ability to make rational choices. Learning to manage these emotions and seek support from loved ones or professionals can lead to more confident and effective decision-making.

Furthermore, recognizing the importance of preventative measures is crucial in health-related decision-making. Taking proactive steps to maintain our health, such as engaging in regular exercise, eating a balanced diet, and getting recommended screenings, can drastically reduce the need for complex decisions in the future.

Ultimately, health-related decision-making is an ongoing process that requires continuous learning and adaptation. It is essential to stay informed about new developments in healthcare and regularly reassess our choices to ensure they align with our evolving needs and circumstances.

By embracing the power of choice in health-related decision-making, we can take control of our well-being and actively shape our future. Whether it is choosing a healthy lifestyle, seeking appropriate medical care, or making treatment decisions, the ability to make informed choices empowers us to lead healthier and happier lives.

Decision-Making for Personal Growth and Happiness

Making decisions is an essential part of our lives. From the moment we wake up in the morning until we go to bed at night, we are constantly faced with choices that shape our future. Whether big or small, these decisions have the power to impact our personal growth and ultimately determine our happiness.

In the subchapter "Decision-Making for Personal Growth and Happiness" of the book "The Power of Choice: Empowering Everyone's Decision-Making," we delve into the profound impact that our choices have on our lives. This section is addressed to everyone, regardless of their background, age, or beliefs, as decision-making is a universal aspect of the human experience.

The subchapter begins by exploring the significance of decision-making in personal growth. Each decision we make, whether it is related to our careers, relationships, or health, has the potential to shape who we become. By understanding the power of our choices, we can actively pursue personal growth and create a life filled with purpose and meaning.

Furthermore, the subchapter delves into the relationship between decision-making and happiness. It emphasizes the importance of aligning our decisions with our values and desires. When we make choices that are in line with our true selves, we experience a deep sense of fulfillment and joy. Moreover, we discuss how decision-making can impact our overall well-being, as making choices that prioritize self-care and mental health can lead to a happier and more balanced life.

To aid the readers in their decision-making journey, the subchapter offers practical tips and strategies. It explores various decision-making frameworks, such as the pros and cons method, the cost-benefit analysis, and the intuition-based approach. By providing these tools, readers can feel more empowered and confident in their decision-making abilities.

Ultimately, "Decision-Making for Personal Growth and Happiness" aims to inspire readers to take control of their lives and make choices that align with their aspirations and values. It encourages them to embrace the power of choice and view decision-making as an opportunity for growth and happiness.

No matter where you are in life, this subchapter will provide you with the guidance and insights needed to make decisions that foster personal growth and lead to a happier, more fulfilling life. Remember, the power to choose is in your hands.

Chapter 9: Empowering Everyone's Decision-Making

Promoting Decision-Making Skills in Education

In today's fast-paced and ever-changing world, the ability to make effective decisions is a crucial skill that everyone needs. Whether you are a student, parent, teacher, or professional, the power of choice plays a significant role in shaping our lives. This subchapter will delve into the importance of promoting decision-making skills in education and how it can empower individuals in various aspects of life.

Education is not just about acquiring knowledge; it is about equipping individuals with the skills and tools they need to navigate through life successfully. Decision-making is one such skill that needs to be fostered from an early age. By promoting decision-making skills in education, we empower individuals to become confident, independent thinkers who can make sound choices.

One of the primary benefits of promoting decision-making skills in education is that it encourages critical thinking. When students are exposed to situations that require decision-making, they learn to analyze information, consider alternatives, and evaluate potential outcomes. This process helps to develop their analytical and problem-solving abilities, which are vital in today's complex world.

Furthermore, promoting decision-making skills in education helps individuals become more self-aware. By engaging in decision-making processes, individuals gain a deeper understanding of their values, beliefs, and goals. This self-awareness enables them to align their decisions with their personal and professional aspirations, leading to a more fulfilling and purpose-driven life.

In addition to enhancing critical thinking and self-awareness, promoting decision-making skills in education equips individuals with resilience and adaptability. Life is full of uncertainties, and the ability to make effective decisions in the face of challenges is crucial. By providing students with opportunities to practice decision-making, we prepare them to tackle unexpected situations and adapt to changing circumstances.

Promoting decision-making skills in education is not limited to the classroom; it extends to all niches of life. Whether you are a parent guiding your child's choices, a professional facing career decisions, or an individual making personal choices, honing your decision-making skills is essential for success and happiness.

In conclusion, promoting decision-making skills in education is paramount in empowering individuals to lead fulfilling lives. By fostering critical thinking, self-awareness, and adaptability, individuals become confident decision-makers who can navigate through life's challenges with ease. Whether you are a student or a professional, the power of choice is in your hands, and by embracing it, you can shape your destiny.

Building Decision-Making Communities

In a world filled with countless choices and decisions, it is essential to understand the power of building decision-making communities. The ability to make informed and effective choices is a skill that affects every aspect of our lives, from personal relationships to professional endeavors. By creating communities that support and empower individuals in their decision-making processes, we can enhance our collective ability to make choices that align with our values and goals.

The concept of decision-making communities centers around the idea that individuals can benefit from the wisdom and experiences of others. When faced with a difficult decision, seeking input and guidance from a community of like-minded individuals can provide fresh perspectives and insights that may have otherwise been overlooked. These communities can be formed in various ways, such as through online forums, support groups, or even close-knit circles of friends and family.

One of the key benefits of building decision-making communities is the opportunity for shared learning. Each decision we make is an opportunity to expand our knowledge and understanding of the world. By engaging with others who have faced similar choices, we can gain valuable insights and learn from their experiences. This collective wisdom can help us navigate complex decisions with greater confidence and clarity.

Moreover, decision-making communities foster a sense of accountability and support. When we involve others in our decision-making processes, we not only gain different perspectives but also develop a network of individuals who are invested in our success. This support network can provide encouragement, guidance, and even hold us accountable for the choices we make. By actively participating in decision-making communities, we can create a strong foundation for personal growth and development.

Furthermore, decision-making communities can serve as a source of inspiration and motivation. Seeing others overcome challenges and make bold choices can inspire us to step out of our comfort zones and pursue our aspirations. The stories and experiences shared within these communities can ignite our own passions and drive us towards making decisions that align with our authentic selves.

In conclusion, building decision-making communities is a powerful tool for empowering everyone's decision-making. By engaging with others, we can tap into a wealth of knowledge, gain new perspectives, and receive the support needed to make informed choices. These communities can serve as a catalyst for personal growth, inspire us to take risks, and ultimately lead us towards a more fulfilling and purpose-driven life. So, let us embrace the power of decision-making communities and unlock our full potential in making choices that shape our lives.

Encouraging Inclusive Decision-Making Processes

In today's fast-paced and interconnected world, the ability to make effective decisions is paramount to success. Whether it's choosing a career path, making financial decisions, or deciding on personal matters, our lives are filled with countless choices. However, the process of decision-making can sometimes be overwhelming, especially when faced with complex or uncertain situations.

This subchapter aims to shed light on the importance of inclusive decision-making processes and how they can empower individuals from all walks of life to make better choices. By embracing inclusivity, we can harness the collective wisdom and diverse perspectives of a wide range of people, ultimately leading to more informed and thoughtful decisions.

Inclusive decision-making is about ensuring that everyone's voice is heard and taken into account. It goes beyond merely seeking input from a diverse group of individuals; it involves creating an environment where everyone feels comfortable expressing their opinions and ideas without fear of judgment or exclusion. This inclusive approach fosters a sense of ownership and collective responsibility, enhancing the overall quality of decision-making.

One key aspect of encouraging inclusive decision-making processes is actively seeking out diverse perspectives. This can be achieved by involving people from different backgrounds, cultures, and experiences in the decision-making process. By doing so, we can tap into a wealth of knowledge and unique insights that would otherwise be missed. It is important to remember that diversity goes beyond visible differences such as race or gender; it also encompasses diversity of thought, values, and beliefs.

Another crucial element is promoting open and respectful communication. Creating a safe space for individuals to express their ideas and concerns without fear of backlash or ridicule is vital. Encouraging active listening and valuing each person's contribution fosters an environment where everyone feels valued and respected. This inclusive communication style helps to build trust and understanding among decision-makers, leading to better collaboration and ultimately more effective decisions.

Inclusive decision-making processes also involve acknowledging and addressing biases and prejudices that may hinder objective decision-making. By actively challenging our own biases and seeking diverse perspectives, we can mitigate the impact of unconscious biases and ensure fairness and equity in the decision-making process.

In conclusion, encouraging inclusive decision-making processes is essential for empowering everyone to make better choices. By embracing diversity, promoting open communication, and addressing biases, we can harness the collective wisdom and insights of individuals from all walks of life. Inclusive decision-making not only leads to more informed and effective decisions but also fosters a sense of belonging and ownership among decision-makers. By embracing the power of inclusivity, we can unlock the full potential of decision-making and create a more equitable and prosperous future for all.

Chapter 10: Conclusion

Recap of Key Concepts

In this subchapter, we will recap some of the key concepts covered in the book "The Power of Choice: Empowering Everyone's Decision-Making." Whether you are a student, a professional, or simply someone interested in improving your decision-making skills, these concepts will help you make informed choices and navigate through life with confidence.

The first concept we discussed is the importance of understanding that making decisions is a fundamental part of our daily lives. Every decision we make, no matter how small or significant, has the potential to shape our future. By recognizing the power of choice, we can take control of our lives and actively create the outcomes we desire.

Next, we emphasized the significance of gathering relevant information before making a decision. It is crucial to seek out various perspectives, conduct research, and consider the potential consequences of each option. By doing so, we can make well-informed choices that align with our values and goals.

Another key concept we explored is the role of intuition in decision-making. While logic and rationality are essential, our gut feelings and instincts can provide valuable insights. Learning to trust your intuition can lead to more confident and authentic decision-making, especially in situations where the information is limited or ambiguous.

We also examined the impact of mindset on decision-making. Adopting a growth mindset, which embraces challenges and sees failure as an opportunity for learning and growth, can enhance your decision-making abilities. By reframing setbacks as learning experiences, you can approach decisions with a positive and resilient attitude.

Lastly, we discussed the importance of taking responsibility for our decisions. Understanding that we have the power to choose empowers us to take ownership of our actions and their consequences. By accepting responsibility for our decisions, we can learn from mistakes, adapt, and make better choices in the future.

In conclusion, this subchapter serves as a recap of the key concepts covered in "The Power of Choice: Empowering Everyone's Decision-Making." By understanding the importance of decision-making, gathering relevant information, trusting our intuition, adopting a growth mindset, and taking responsibility, we can enhance our decision-making skills and lead more fulfilling lives. Remember, the power of choice lies within each and every one of us, and by harnessing it effectively, we can shape our destinies and achieve our dreams.

The Ongoing Journey of Empowered Decision-Making

In the fast-paced world we live in, making decisions has become a constant part of our daily lives. From small choices like what to wear or what to eat, to life-altering ones such as choosing a career or a life partner, decision-making shapes our future and determines the paths we take. However, the process of making decisions can often be overwhelming, leaving many of us feeling uncertain and anxious about the outcomes. It is here that the ongoing journey of empowered decision-making becomes crucial.

Empowered decision-making is about taking control of our choices, understanding the power we hold, and embracing the responsibility that comes with it. It is a continuous journey that requires self-reflection, self-awareness, and a commitment to personal growth. This subchapter delves into the various aspects of this ongoing journey and provides insights and tools to navigate through the decision-making process with confidence and clarity.

One of the key elements of empowered decision-making is understanding our values and priorities. By aligning our choices with our core values, we can ensure that our decisions are in harmony with our authentic selves. This subchapter explores various techniques for identifying our values, such as self-assessment exercises and reflection prompts, helping readers gain a deeper understanding of their own beliefs and principles.

Another crucial aspect of the ongoing journey of empowered decision-making is developing effective decision-making strategies. This subchapter provides practical frameworks and techniques to enhance decision-making skills, such as the pros and cons analysis, decision matrices, and the power of intuition. It also emphasizes the importance of gathering relevant information, seeking advice from trusted sources, and considering the potential consequences of our choices.

Furthermore, this subchapter explores the role of self-confidence and self-trust in empowered decision-making. It encourages readers to cultivate a positive mindset, embrace their intuition, and believe in their ability to make sound choices. It also addresses the fear of making mistakes and provides strategies for overcoming decision paralysis.

Throughout this subchapter, the readers are reminded that the journey of empowered decision-making is not a one-time event but a continuous process. It highlights the importance of learning from past decisions, adapting to changing circumstances, and embracing the growth opportunities that decision-making offers.

The ongoing journey of empowered decision-making is a lifelong endeavor that can transform our lives and empower us to create the future we desire. By understanding the power of choice and embracing the responsibility it entails, we can navigate through life with confidence, clarity, and a sense of purpose. This subchapter serves as a guide for everyone seeking to enhance their decision-making skills and embark on their own journey towards empowerment.

Inspiring Others to Embrace the Power of Choice

In today's fast-paced and ever-changing world, decision-making has become a crucial skill that everyone must possess. Whether it's choosing a career path, making important life choices, or even deciding what to have for lunch, the power of choice plays a significant role in shaping our lives. This subchapter aims to inspire and empower individuals from all walks of life to embrace the power of choice and make confident decisions.

Making decisions can be daunting and overwhelming for many. The fear of making the wrong choice or the uncertainty of the outcome often holds people back from taking the necessary steps forward. However, by understanding the potential and impact of our choices, we can unlock a world of opportunities and personal growth.

The power of choice lies within each and every one of us. It is the ability to take control of our lives and make decisions that align with our values, desires, and goals. It is about recognizing that we have the power to shape our own destinies, instead of being at the mercy of circumstances.

To inspire others to embrace the power of choice, we must first help them understand the importance of self-awareness. By knowing ourselves better – our strengths, weaknesses, values, and aspirations – we can make choices that are authentic and true to who we are. This self-discovery process allows us to tap into our passions and purpose, making decision-making a more fulfilling and meaningful experience.

Furthermore, it is vital to encourage individuals to view decision-making as an opportunity for growth and learning. Every choice we make, regardless of the outcome, provides valuable lessons and insights. By reframing failures as stepping stones to success, we can empower others to take risks, learn from their experiences, and continuously improve their decision-making abilities.

Lastly, we should emphasize the importance of taking responsibility for our choices. Every decision we make has consequences, and it is essential to own up to them. By accepting responsibility, we empower ourselves to learn from our mistakes, adapt, and make better choices in the future.

In conclusion, inspiring others to embrace the power of choice is about empowering individuals to take control of their lives, make confident decisions, and embrace the journey of personal growth. By fostering self-awareness, encouraging a growth mindset, and promoting responsibility, we can empower everyone to realize the potential within themselves and make choices that lead to a more fulfilling and purposeful life.

Milton Keynes UK
Ingram Content Group UK Ltd.
UKHW020625291123
433416UK00016B/1069